A PRAYER WARRIOR'S
WEAPONS *of* WAR

RESCUING
THE LOST,
STALKED & PRODIGALS

KERRY E. GARNER

A Prayer Warrior's Weapons of War: Rescuing the Lost, Stalked & Prodigals

ISBN Paperback #979-8-9867266-7-0

ISBN ebook #979-8-9867266-8-7

Copyright © 2025 by Kerry E. Garner

Tulsa, OK 74133

Reach us via email: kerryegarner@gmail.com

Instagram @Kerryelisabethgarner

Cover Design and Typesetting: Jennifer Grisham

Editorial Consultant: Shannon McCoy & Audrey Reeves

Contents

Acknowledgments

First and foremost, I want to acknowledge my precious Savior, Jesus Christ, my loving Father God, and the precious Holy Spirit. I am a nobody in and of myself. But as His daughter, I was led to write our story of victory. My children were saved because of God's love, provision, authority, and guidance. I am so very grateful. To my grandparents in heaven, I love you and appreciate how you represented God and were true oaks of righteousness in my life. To my beloved husband Frank, we were just eighteen-year-old kids when we met at ORU. Thank you for being strong and courageous and pushing me to keep moving. Thank you for giving me wisdom, guidance, and provision. I truly adore you. To my greatest gifts, Brandon, Emily, Brad, Julia, Bennett & Andy, my heart is so overwhelmed with the goodness of God when I think of you. Your encouragement, support, and love is a priceless gift. You all inspire me to be a watchman on the wall! You are my treasures, and I love you. Being Mama and Mimi to you is my greatest joy. To my daddy, I appreciate the strong roots and love that you instilled in me. Thank you for teaching me Jesus in my earliest years. Momma, a pillar of grace and anointed beauty, I am forever thankful to have had you as a shining example of God's faithfulness. To my stepfather, David, thank you for being a rock to our sweet momma and us. Skip, thank you for always being present to share the love of Jesus, sound wisdom, God's

Word, and a hug. Kevin, when I was a lost, hurting teenager, your example, strength, and courage truly brought me through one of the most challenging moments of my life. John Paul, you were the first to teach me how to love like a Momma. Though just your big sis, when you joined our family, I developed a desire to nurture, love, and protect as never before. And to my Jenny, my best friend....I don't have words to express what you are to me: a spirit-led rock, a laugh until it hurts, and squeeze you through the pain, sister. You are such a precious gift to me.

To my beloved family, thank you for always having my back and giving me much love, strength, wisdom, and guidance. Uncle Bruce, Aunt Susie, Uncle Dodd, Aunt Becca, Ben, Jim, Mary Beth, Shane, Laurie, Leslie, Doug, Leila Margaret, Elise, Marty, Chelsea Paige, Hunter, Cole, Megan, Henry, Maggie, Tony, Lynn, Matt, Lauren, Anne, Vinnie, Jackie, Santino, Domenica, Gale, Scott, Momma Anne, Merry and Jack: I pray for you daily. You are all so valuable beyond words. I love each of you.

Through God's mighty men and women who were brave and obedient enough to preach, teach, and proclaim His truths, I have been spiritually "marked" by your lives. I could never name them all, it would be too many, but I do want to give a few shout-outs to some who pull me up higher in the things of God: Frank, Brandon, Brad, Bill, Bettianne, Billy Joe, Sharon, Oral, Evelyn, Sammy, Delicia, Kevin, David, Francie, Kenneth C., Gloria, Billye, Amanda, Kenneth H., Robin D., Robin, Kat, Dutch, Bill, Fran, Carl Jon, Richard, Lindsay, Cheryl, Charles, Marty, Jenny, Shannon, Kelly, Kellykat, Rosa, Mandy, Charlotte, Sharon, Willie, Paul, Ashley, Kirk, Phil, Cathie, George,

Acknowledgments

Terri, Hank, Kent, Lisa, Robert, Nancy, Bill W. and Joyce. And to my besties, my ladies' group, my cohorts, and the true treasures of my life, thank you for loving me so well. May God bless you all! Lastly, thank you to Shannon McCoy and Audrey Reeves for editing this book and to my sister Jenny for designing the beautiful cover and for both proofing and typesetting it.

Introduction

The lost, stalked, and prodigals of this generation need us to rescue them from some very dark places. Jesus did His part. Now, it is time for us to take our place as the sons and daughters of the Most High God and go rescue them. The truth is, as Christians, you are constantly the target of Satan; sometimes more subtly, but other times, Wham!, right in your face. The consequences of Satan's attacks leave God's people in piles of rubble. It leaves families as only burned-out shells. Defeated is not what God called us to be. Jesus died on the cross so that we would have a *victorious* life and not a life of running from evil, hiding in caves. He has provided us with specific weapons to use when rescuing our people from demonic assignments set for them.

I speak from experience. Our story is not a story of a prodigal. Yet, it still holds the same weapons that can be used to successfully rescue your children, your family members, and the lost from all demonic assignments and traps set for them. Growing up, I experienced firsthand the aftermath of having a bomb dropped on my family. Then, as an adult mama bear, our family had to fight for the life of both of my beloved boys. I am writing this book from a sheer place of wanting to help others the way God helped us. I am not a psychologist, so this book is written in practical, everyday language. My heart knows the extreme desperation to rescue one's children or loved ones. Trust me, there is hope!

My husband and I have the honor of being the parents of two incredible sons. We took this job seriously. We understood that our precious boys were a gift, and we endeavored to raise them knowing Jesus as their Saviour and walking in the fullness thereof. Even though we had them grounded in the Word, there were holes in our preparations that left us vulnerable as a family. And the crazy thing is, we were going through life thinking everything was perfect until it was *not*!

You may be in a similar situation, needing help rescuing your children from a dark existence far from who they were created to be by God. Their identity seems lost or missing. Or, you may be a Christian who understands that you have been charged with going after lost souls, and you want some insight.

God provides us with strategic keys to rescue people, and we must do our part. In the following chapters, you will be given the weapons to help! As believers and co-laborers of Christ, we can reach our loved ones in many ways. God forbid if we don't try all of them with all diligence! I went outside of my church circle to find help for my sons. Love does not stay in a religious box. Stay within the bounds of what your Bible says, and follow the Holy Spirit to rescue your people. My sons were rescued, and I intend to see the rest of my lost family come to have a relationship with Christ. And I am not stopping there. My heart is to fulfill the ministry He gave to every believer. I am sharing everything I have learned thus far to help you, too. Let us go get our people! All glory be to our Savior!

2 Cor. 5:17-19

Therefore, if anyone is in Christ, he is a new creation; old things have passed away; behold, all things have become new. Now all things are of God, who has reconciled us to Himself through Jesus Christ and has given us the ministry of reconciliation.

Chapter One

Understanding the "Why?"

Many people get stuck in the mud pit of "Why me? Why is this happening to me? Why am I being targeted?" You do not understand the big picture, and, in ignorance, you allow Satan to wreak havoc on you and your loved ones.

Satan can see anointing. He doesn't know what God will use that anointing for, but he knows when people have it. Satan knows the ones who have it strongly. He knows families who have a strong calling. His goal is to knock you off your place or get you so caught up in yourself that you cannot fulfill the call of God on your life. What is the answer to why you are being attacked or why your child or loved one is being hit? You are God's, and Satan wants to stop you. Period.

Remember, you are made in the image of God. In John 10:10, Jesus says, "The thief does not come except to steal, and to kill, and to destroy. I have come that they may have life and that they may have it more abundantly." Satan hates you because you are God's workmanship — His beloved. You were special enough that God sent His only son to die on the cross to save you. That's how precious you and your children are. If you are a Christian, you are joint heirs with Christ (Romans 8:17). He has given power and authority to you to operate on this Earth. The issue is that people in many churches are not taught how to operate in the authority God has given them. Or they are not taught or are unwilling to lay down the things that will render them powerless in their battle.

While in prayer, I saw an eagle flying over water crying out. It gathered up the demonic assignments in the form of spiders, parasites, snakes, and ticks. Each of these demonic assignments were used by Satan to knock people out of their place. When a demonic assignment was given, they were used by the enemy to get people so self-focused that they were no longer relevant in the war against him. We are to be like the *eagles* of our lives and go after the spiders, parasites, snakes, and ticks that try to poison, attach themselves, kill, or trap us, our spouses, our children, or our people. "He found him in a desert land And the wasteland, a howling wilderness; He encircled him, He instructed him, He kept him as the apple of His eye. As an eagle stirs up its nest, Hovers over its young, Spreading out its wings, taking them up, Carrying them on its wings, So the Lord alone led him, And there was no foreign god with him" (Deuteronomy 32:11-12).

There are many kinds of demonic assignments sent. Some are direct; the people being used are willing participants and know what they are doing, and they just do not care about the damage it does to you as an individual. They want what they want and will use you or your children to get it. Some demonic assignments hit indirectly, like when a daddy has an affair and leaves his family. This hit can have repercussions throughout the family, friendships, and even churches. Sometimes, these assignments are sent to latch onto you like a tick (or stalker) and drain you of all your strength, time, and resources. Some are sent to plant deceptive thoughts in you that are contrary to the Word of God.

Parasites feed off their hosts. Sometimes, the "parasitic" people know that they are being used and are fully aware and are willing to be used. Other times, from deception or lack of knowledge, they don't know. In any case, it is your responsibility to listen to the Holy Spirit and use the weapons given to you to remove them from your personal, spouse's, children's, and circle's lives. In the case of adults, if you are targeted, find trustworthy people grounded in the Word to take counsel from and to cover you with their prayers. Rely on the Holy Spirit and follow peace. These parasites are seducing. They are alluring. Their goal is to put you in bondage or destroy you. These seducing spirits are sent after people in the form of demonic assignments.

In 1 Peter 5:8, the Word says, "Be sober, be vigilant; because your adversary the devil walks about like a roaring lion, seeking whom he may devour." One of our biggest failures as the people of God is not truly understanding how much *Satan will so actively pursue us to knock us out of what God has for us.* He is an aggressively active enemy. We need to be just as aggressively watching, defending, and taking ground for God!

Okay, now stop, take a minute, and breathe. Let me say this: God did NOT leave us defenseless. He gave us definite weapons in his Word to defend against these demonic assignments. Satan will come after you, but as it says in Romans 8:31, "If God is for us, who can be against us?" Both of my children were set free from the demonic assignments that came after them, and in this book, you will be given keys to the pathway to freedom for yourself, your children, and your people.

We are going to begin here. You may be at the place of not knowing where to start. You have exhausted all your avenues, and all possible solutions have been met with denial, resistance, or misunderstanding. But God! The Bible says, If any of you lacks wisdom, let him ask of God, who gives to all liberally and without reproach, and it will be given to him (James 1:5 NKJV). Quite simply, ask God for wisdom. Then, listen to what He tells you. In the quiet leadings, you will find clues to unlocking the prison that your loved one is trapped in. God did it for us and will do it for you! If it is you personally who has found yourself trapped or stalked, God will give you a way of escape. At times, you will see the results immediately, but sometimes, it is a process. Small victories add up to complete freedom.

I will give you a prayer, often called the Ephesians prayer, that I pray over myself and my family daily. You may not have heard of them, but Paul prayed these words to ask for a spirit of wisdom and understanding, so it is the perfect place to start to set you up for success. It's a heart posture before God. I also believe you need to pray this out loud. Your faith will grow as you hear the Word. There is such power in the spoken Word of God (*see* Romans 10:17).

Ephesian's Prayer:

God of our Lord Jesus Christ, the Father of glory, may give to (*name yourself and the person needing set free*) the spirit of wisdom and revelation in the knowledge of Him, (let) the eyes of (our) understanding being enlightened; that (we) may know what is the hope of His calling, what are the riches of the glory of His inheritance in the saints, and what is the exceeding greatness of His power toward us who believe, according to the working of His mighty power which He worked in Christ when He raised Him from the dead and seated Him at His right hand in the heavenly places, far above all principality, and power and might and dominion, and every name that is named, not only in this age but also in that which is to come. And He put all things under His feet, and gave Him to be head over all things to the church, And you, He made alive, who were dead in trespasses and sins, But God, who is rich in mercy, because of His great love with which He loved us, even when we

were dead in trespasses, made us alive together with Christ (by grace you have been saved), and raised us up together, and made us sit together in the heavenly places in Christ Jesus (Ephesians 1:17-22, 2:1, 4-6).

In Jesus's Name I pray,

Amen.

Chapter Two

Dead Man Walking: Our Story

The circumstances we found ourselves in are what I would now call a strategic, well-planned hit on my family. In 2019, my eldest son, Brandon, had just started medical school. He felt something weird in his throat, and long story short, it ended up being cancer. This development, in itself, would have been enough to face. I will go into the depths of his healing journey in the future, but this book will give you an understanding of how Satan will double down and triple down on you. I will say that through this fire, God never left us and has restored and completely healed Brandon and blessed him despite the attack. He is healed, whole, and a strong example of God's faithfulness. You may also say, well, my child is not going through this, so I cannot identify. Here are the facts. Every child lost can be found! Take the strategic steps we discovered from God's Word, glean from them, and apply them to your situation. You absolutely will see God move on your behalf! My sons are now fully restored, and both are married and strong in their faith.

My younger son, Brad, finished his last two years of high school academically and athletically at the top of his class. He went off to college as a pre-med student, and that is where the bottom fell out. It was not all at once but a slow fade. Entering college, he was a very outgoing, smiley, happy, quick-witted person who always had a pep in his step. I watched my golden retriever son slowly retreat into himself until he was a shell of the boy I once knew — like a dead man walking. What I mean by that is that he would come to our family nights with our whole family, and instead of engaging, talking, and laughing like he used to, he would sit there with a blank stare. When we went to his grandparent's house, a place that usually brought out the fun side of him, he'd sit to the side and not talk. The life that used to be behind his eyes was gone, and we were not sure what had happened. His lifelong friends and his love of fishing and other activities left, too. My husband, my oldest son, his aunt and uncles, his cousins, and his grandparents were discussing behind his back, "What happened to Brad? What's going on? What do we do?"

And let me just say the mama bear in me had already been activated and praying for his brother battling cancer. The warning signs were most likely there earlier with Brad, but I was so distracted with Brandon that I didn't see it thoroughly until it was right in my face. Of course, Satan came to me and started accusing me of my major mama failure of not protecting him earlier or not seeing the signs earlier to help him. I am so thankful for the grace of God.

Remember, the goal of Satan is to destroy you. And it is up to us to be wise to the cunning ways that Satan will use to get us off the course God has set for us. We, as a family, went to God and prayed. Prayer is a key here. We prayed for wisdom and understanding. The Holy Spirit will reveal things to you step by step and layer by layer. In our case, Brad's grandfather had some insight that rang in my spirit as a key. Remember, you must stay open to listening to the Holy Spirit. Grandpa told us how, many years ago, this one person targeted his aunt, who had been a missionary. His aunt had gone into a shell and became very withdrawn. (Sounded familiar!) He told us how his mom had gone and rescued her sister and brought her to their house for her to recover. Eventually, she was able to see the harm of that friendship. I knew that a young man had befriended Brad, but I could not put my finger on what was happening. I just knew there was something unhealthy about the friendship. The young man was a Christian, so I put off my reservations because I did not recognize that Satan often will use Christians to knock you off your path. What? Did I say that? Absolutely. It happens quite often. I'll address this more in the next chapter.

Praying in the Holy Spirit is vital here. Because when you are unsure what is going on, you are unsure how to pray. But the Holy Spirit knows with pin-point accuracy what to pray! By praying in the Spirit, He will target specific things you do not know anything about. He will also drop insight into your heart about the situation. I felt led to listen to a lady that I came across on social media. This mother was telling a story about how her teenage daughter had gone dead behind her eyes. I paid close attention to see if there would be insight into helping with our situation, and there was. She shared how her daughter quit interacting with her family. Again, it sounded very familiar. The girl's father said that he prayed and felt like the Holy Spirit told him to have his daughter leave her phone in their room at night. The girl ended up getting very upset by this request. After many tears, the daughter finally confessed that a friend had confided in her that she was contemplating suicide, and she asked this teenage girl to be on 24-hour "call" to keep her alive. And she made her promise not to tell anyone.

It was like the Holy Spirit turned a light on inside me. I am not saying that this friend of Brad's was suicidal. Brad has never told me what this friend was dealing with. I am saying that our super kindhearted kids can often be targeted, taken advantage of, and manipulated by people. Religious or deceptive spirits often disguise themselves and speak through friends, leaders, social media, counselors, and teachers. They say falsehoods and sow deceptive words and thoughts that directly attack that person's identity. They plant confusion in God's people. This is one reason that we should stay in the Word. The Word will filter out the truth from the lies.

Sometimes, our children are asked to give counsel beyond their ability to help. My now daughter-in-law, Emily, told me that happened to her a few times. Friends would come to her and ask for help because they were feeling suicidal or depressed and wanted her help to keep them alive but not to tell anyone. She told them, "No, I am sorry, I am not equipped for that. I can pray for you, but we need to get you help from an adult." Her parents had set her up with sound wisdom on how to handle this situation. Abuse comes in many forms. Whether physically, mentally, or psychologically, Satan will slither his way in order to abuse and corrupt God's people. Many times, it comes under a veil of secrecy. A "please" and a "promise" not to tell anyone status." Warning! Warning!

Remember, however the "take-down" of your loved one happened, whatever avenue was used, *it is not a place for you to get stuck in reasoning.* Stay at the feet of Jesus. Stay focused on your goal. Brad loved God, and we knew that God would help us. Though Brad did not see what we were saying about his friendship as accurate, his heart posture towards God allowed him to get to where he could be set free. He eventually walked out of that hellish situation. There were definite things we did as a family to stand for him. I will be sharing those with you. Brad was, thankfully, on the right path and healing. Then, a young lady we will call Sarah walked into his life, and this is where Satan doubled down on him.

Brad started dating a beautiful Christian girl who seemingly loved God as much as he did. His entire dating relationship with her was around five or six months. After a couple of months of dating and every month after this, Brad would say to his dad, his brother, and me at the dinner table, "I think I am going to break up with Sarah." But then, when he would return from going out with her, he would tell us that he did not break up. This scenario happened over and over again. We started joking with him, saying, "Come on, Brad, you can do this." Finally, near Christmas break, he heard God loud and clear to end the relationship. He left to meet her at a restaurant and did not come home for five hours! When he finally did come home, we asked what had taken so long, and he told us that she would not let him leave. She had stood in the doorway of his truck and would not let him go.

The situation only intensified. Sarah did not go home for Christmas; instead, she wrote him hundreds of long, drawn-out texts that came in hour by hour and minute by minute. Understand, Brad's brother was undergoing the first of his three surgeries to remove tumors from his throat, so it was pretty ruthless. She would call and leave long voicemails. She made a YouTube channel of why he was so horrible for breaking up with her. At college, she would physically hold onto him to try to prevent him from going to his college classes. During this time, covid hit, and all the students were sent home to finish the year. She chose the apartments right beside our house to move into. She befriended all of his friends to pull info about him. She followed him to four churches, always trying to sit near him. He would go to different coffee shops to study, and she would show up no matter where he went. He loved to play volleyball, and she would show up and try to get on his team. She said she wanted all her things back, which he gave her, but then she returned them and left them at our front door. He did not want them, and she said she did not, so we donated them (sweatshirts and t-shirts). He then got accused of throwing out things she wanted. Day after day, the attacks were a straight-out hit on his character and him as a person.

The circumstances went from the bizarre to the ridiculous. That is a key thing to note. *Do not try to make sense out of and get into arguments with demonically-influenced people.* We never felt his life was in danger, but if we had, we would have filed a restraining order against her. The pursuit was brutal, targeted, and without restraint. I'm not going to go into all the details, but just note that it persisted for an entire year and a half. Church leaders did not believe him or help. Perhaps they did not know how. He did find two groups of friends who protected him from her, and I am incredibly grateful. The true friends who stood up to her when she would call for information on him are so important and valued. The situation we found ourselves in was a mountain that needed moving. What does the Word of God have to say about this?

Mark 11:23

For assuredly, I say to you, whoever says to this mountain, 'Be removed and be cast into the sea,' and does not doubt in his heart, but believes that those things he says will be done, he will have whatever he says.

Matthew 17:20

I say to you, if you have faith as a mustard seed, you will say to this mountain, 'Move from here to there,' and it will move; and nothing will be impossible for you.

Remember, we were standing at the same time for my other son's healing from cancer, and in the same way we were standing in faith for Brandon's healing, we had to activate our faith to believe for Brad's deliverance. We needed God's divine power and wisdom — and quickly. Faith was the key here. The Bible says that "faith comes by hearing, and hearing by the word of God" (Romans:10:17). It also says in James 1:5, "If any of you lacks wisdom, let him ask of God, who gives to all liberally and without reproach, and it will be given to him."

If you are at this point, the place of not understanding what you are up against but knowing that it is a huge giant that needs to be conquered. Here is a prayer you can pray to start the process toward deliverance. It is a simple prayer, but that is the beautiful thing about Jesus. He requires little eloquence. He just needs you to lean into Him, and He will lead you to freedom for yourself or for your loved one.

Prayer of Faith

Dear heavenly Father, I come before you as your servant and child. I am not sure what is going on, but I know that whatever and whomever it is, You have provided a way of escape for (<u>Name of person needing freedom</u>). I asked for your wisdom, and I take it by faith.

In Jesus's Name I pray,

Amen.

Chapter Three

Let's Talk About the Stalk

Okay, let's get down to some weapons used against us. There are many ways that Satan will come after you. Some methods include addiction, depression, intellectualism, pride, ignorance, rejection, lust, abandonment, hurt, bitterness, deception, abuse, shame, and unforgiveness. Whether a subtle or a brutal attack, God did not and does not leave us defenseless. It's essential to be "wise as serpents and innocent as doves." One of my biggest failures as a parent was not understanding that Christians can be used to knock you out of the path that God has set for you. Even Peter, one of Jesus's disciples, rebuked Jesus for saying that He would be killed and then resurrected on the third day. This encounter is recorded in Matthew

16:22-23; we read, "Then Peter took Him aside and began to rebuke Him, saying, "Far be it from You, Lord; this shall not happen to You!" But He turned and said to Peter, "Get behind Me, Satan! You are an offense to Me, for you are not mindful of the things of God, but the things of men." I did not understand that another person who was serving the Lord could be used to usurp you or move you out of God's plan. And in my not understanding, this led to pitfalls for myself and my child that could have been avoided.

Satan will use other Christian people to knock you out of your God-given purpose. Period! This fact is something not often spoken about or taught. And in that vacuum, there are many trapped. We think or mistakenly believe that other Christians — whether friends, leaders, pastors, family, spouses, girlfriends, boyfriends, and teachers have our best interest at heart. Here is where putting people on a pedestal can leave you spinning. Sometimes, others have marred intentions because of a stronghold they are struggling with or a wrong belief system. That is why we need the Holy Spirit. He cuts through all the hogwash and separates people's persona from the true intention of their hearts. The Holy Spirit will give us warnings, and it is up to us to heed those warnings.

Once, in the early days of my ministry, I had a lady come to my Bible study that God had me start a few years earlier. Because she was gifted with spiritual gifts that I did not have, and because she was beautiful, charismatic, and would often speak of what God said to her, I started listening to a voice that was not God that said, "You do not measure up." Over the course of time, this lady came to me and said that she, not me, really should be the leader of my Bible study group. Because I was not grounded in who God made me to be and because I had been entertaining what the enemy had been whispering to me, I gave away something precious that God had called me to do. I am not saying that she was not called to women's ministry or that she was evil. If God gives you something precious, guard it with all diligence. Forfeiting an assignment is giving away part of what you were called to do. I agreed with her request. I went home and cried. I was devastated because I truly loved each of these ladies, and I loved teaching them from God's Word. Demonic voices can influence Christian and non-Christian people. The Holy Spirit is given to us to see clearly. The lady started teaching things that would give me checks in my spirit. It was not God's best. God told me to walk away, and I did. It grieved me so much. I asked forgiveness for allowing someone to take from me what He had purposed me to lead. I had to forgive her. After about six months, God led me to start a new group. A few of my previous Bible study ladies also came, but God added some true gems I am so blessed to do life with today. Restoration is a beautiful thing!

Side note here: God can recalculate you or your loved one. Do not get lost in the details of what should have been. What I mean by that is, just like when you are driving and get off course, the navigation system can recalculate and get you back on course when you repent. God can give resurrection life to the dead things. We need to trust Him as our loving Father to have our best interest at heart and to follow His leading.

When your calling challenges unrenewed people, they often react by doubling down on you through threats, rules, accusations, and lies. In 1 Kings 19:1, we find the ungodly King Ahab went to his wife, Queen Jezebel, and told her that the prophet Elijah had gotten rid of the idols in the land and had killed 450 of the false prophets of Baal! *Jezebel was threatened by Elijah.* In her response to that threat, Jezebel sent a message to Elijah saying, "So let the gods do to me, and more also, if I do not make your life as the life of one of them(the dead false prophets) by tomorrow about this time." She threatens to cut his head off, destroy his ministry, and assassinate his character. Even though he had just come off a great victory for God, one person's threat sent him running, hiding under a tree, thinking it would be easier to die than to face the one threatening him. He eventually went to a cave where he could calm down and hear God. When you are being stalked, you can feel fear. It can be scary and intimidating when someone threatens to kill you, destroy you, cut off your friendships and family, destroy your character, or cause harm to you or your family. If you are watching it from the outside, it can be scary, too. Here's the thing: God did not leave us defenseless! And we must put our faith over that fear. "For God has not given us a spirit of fear, but of power and of love and a sound mind" (2 Timothy 1:7).

Fear opens the door to Satan because when you tolerate fear, you are contaminated by it. It leaves a foothold or legal right for Satan to come in and trap you or your loved one. Fear, itself, becomes a trap. The Bible says in Proverbs 29:25 that the "Fear of Man proves to be a snare, but whoever trusts in the Lord is kept safe." Okay, let us look at this from two sides of the coin. If your Christian child, who loves to help people, is a people pleaser, then whatever it takes to win other people's approval, they will bow to. Once they have bowed to it, they can easily be controlled by it and often submit their calling to it. On the other side of the coin, if you are a people pleaser, then despite the checks you are getting from God about the dangers, you often brush those warnings aside because they look innocent or harmless in your head. You end up submitting your calling to them. Live for the approval of one God. Living for the approval of anyone else is a trap. Trust in what God says about you and who He says you are, and walk in the fear of the Lord. *Recognize that God did not create you to be controlled by anyone else.*

Quick side note — please go to the police or authorities if you are in a dangerous situation or if the person you are trying to save is in a life-threatening circumstance. Just like we went to the doctor when Brandon was facing a cancer battle, you need to follow the law of the land and use wisdom in the natural. This book does not tell you how to proceed on the judicial side of things but how to attack it from the spiritual warfare side. These two can work together. And honestly, however and whomever God wants to use to save you or your loved ones is just perfect.

True love, the God kind of love, whether coming from a pastor, parent, leader, friend, girlfriend, boyfriend, or spouse, will want to protect you from harm. A love tainted with a demonic assignment will use control, guilt, force, mockery, and other manipulation and control to get what they want above what God wants for you. Inviting the Holy Spirit into your life is important because He was given to us by God to help us through these unreadable and even dangerous moments in life. If Brad had heeded the leading of the Holy Spirit when He initially told Brad to break up with Sarah, then a lot of heartache could have been avoided. If I had heeded the voice of the Holy Spirit telling me not to give up my ladies' group, then I know a lot of my heartache and our other friendships that got negatively affected would have been avoided. Following the Holy Spirit's guidance is vital.

You may identify with this same thing. You have someone in your life who has turned into a different person, not in a good way. If you are left wondering what happened to the person you once knew, let me tell you there is hope! You may be the person who is only a shadow of who you used to be, and you want to find your way out of this craziness. You may be the person who feels like yourself, but everyone around you is saying that you are not the same person. God did not leave you without a solution! Our story is not unique; it's an age-old story of how Satan came to rob, kill, steal, and destroy us. Satan wants you to think it's a hopeless situation because then you'll give up. Here's the secret according to Mark 9:23, "all things are possible to him who believes."

Understand that Satan is strategic — meaning he has a long-term strategy goal of rendering you useless and will use step-by-step tactics to get there. Knowing his goal is to knock you out of your calling, do not be surprised when he hits you from several angles. The exciting thing is that the perspective and wisdom gained after you have won the battle will propel you forward into your God-given destiny. It will take grit, strength, fortitude, a willingness to listen, faith, trust, and obedience. But you will find a miracle of God at the end of the battle if you don't stop advancing. I am so very grateful for a God that cares. And a God that gives us a handbook, the Bible, to overcome anything or anyone Satan throws at us. As we, as a family, were walking through it, there were many questions, and it took God's grace to right and restore the mess.

Chapter Four

Our Secret Weapon Is the Holy Spirit!

Make yourself a pliable, usable vessel that God can work through. If you have never given your heart to Jesus, you need to start there. All the power and authority required will be found within the boundaries of the Christian faith, and there is no other way but through Jesus. As a Christian, you need to access all the weapons and authority God has given to you. It is not a time for lukewarm Christianity. If you have yet to receive the Holy Spirit, also known as the baptism of the Holy Ghost, into your life, you are putting yourself and your loved one at a considerable disadvantage. Here is why. In Acts 2:38, we read, "Then Peter said to them, 'Repent, and let every one of you be baptized in the name of Jesus Christ for the remission of sins, and you shall receive the gift of the Holy Spirit.'" It is the Spirit of God, given to us to help us! Jesus told us this, "And I will pray the Father, and He will give you another Helper, that He may abide with you forever — the Spirit of truth, whom the world cannot receive because it neither sees Him nor knows Him; but you know Him, for He dwells with you and will be in you" (John 14:16-17).

We see here that the Holy Spirit is a Helper. He is the one who will help us out of these awful situations! He is the "Spirit of Truth," in a world full of so many voices, we need the Holy Spirit to lead us. The Holy Spirit is imperative when rescuing our people and getting ourselves out of these circumstances. Why? When we pray in the Holy Spirit, also known as tongues, the Holy Spirit intercedes for us for the things we do not even know to pray. He knows precisely what is needed to help us. In Romans 8:26, the Bible says, "Likewise the Spirit also helps in our weaknesses. For we do not know what we should pray for as we ought, but the Spirit Himself makes intercession for us with groanings which cannot be uttered." After you pray to receive the Holy Spirit, thank Him for filling you. He will drop words or syllables in your heart that are not your own language. It is a special language given to you by the Holy Spirit to receive his wisdom and guidance. Following are both a prayer of Salvation and a prayer to receive the Holy Spirit. Pray in faith that you will receive!

Prayer of Salvation:

Dear Heavenly Father, I come to You in the Name of Jesus. Your Word says in Acts 2:21, "And it shall come to pass that whoever calls on the name of the LORD shall be saved." I am calling on You now, in Your holy Name, Jesus. I ask You to come into my heart and be Lord over my life. Your Word says in Romans 10:9, "that if you confess with your mouth the Lord Jesus and believe in your heart that God has raised Him from the dead, you will be saved." I now confess Jesus is my Lord! I believe in my heart that God raised Him from the dead, and I thank You for saving me.

In Jesus's Name I pray,

Amen.

Prayer of Receiving the Holy Spirit:

And now, as a blood-bought child of God, I ask You to fill me with Your Holy Spirit. In Acts 2:4, it says that "they were all filled with the Holy Spirit and began to speak with other tongues, as the Spirit gave them utterance." I expectantly receive the gift of the Holy Spirit with evidence of speaking in tongues. I receive it now by faith. Thank You, Lord, for filling me.

In Jesus's Name I pray,

Amen.

Rescuing the Lost, Stalked & Prodigals

Chapter 5

Lay Pride Down!

If you are pursuing a lost or ensnared person, religious pride must be laid at Jesus's feet. Nobody, and I mean NOBODY, wants to run and get help from a pride-filled braggart who wants to prove they are right over the desire to help this person. Lay your religious huffiness down and humble yourself before your God. Because, honestly, but for the grace of God, it could be you trapped in some situation. And the love of God, which you are to be operating in, covers a multitude of sins. Be ready to offer a way for the lost loved one to come out of their darkness that is not surrounded by critical eyes, shame, and finger-pointing. Be a safe person, not a jerk.

When my son Brad was going through the first of the two attacks, he could not see the harm in the friendship. He told me later that it made him angry when everyone told him he had changed and was not the same person. He had a pastor whom he loved and respected teach a lesson about pride. He taught that when the people you trust in your life tell you that you have changed negatively, but you do not believe them, you could be in pride. In Proverbs 16:18, the Bible says, "Pride goes before destruction and a haughty spirit before a fall." Pride is an attitude of being independent from God. Brad repented and chose to cut off that friendship. Even though he did not see the harm, he trusted his family. Through this, God saved him from a circumstance meant to harm him.

If the person you are trying to reach is dealing with a stronghold of pride in their life and you have been beating your head against a wall trying to get them to listen to you, know that God gives us keys in his Word to deal with that. I will be addressing that specifically in another chapter.

Chapter Six

Ripping up the Roots!

Unforgiveness and bitterness are huge in keeping people from rescuing or getting free from the traps and demonic assignments set for them. Straight up, it is a legal matter. "Be angry, and do not sin": do not let the sun go down on your wrath, nor give place to the devil" (Ephesians 4:26-27). God tells us that if you keep hold of that anger, you give "place" to the devil. In other words, you provide a loophole for Satan to attack you. I am not saying that what that person did or is currently doing to you or your loved one is correct when you forgive. It may have been a horrendous offense. In forgiving, you are saying that you release the right to hold bitterness and hatred towards them. You are giving it to the One Who is the righteous Judge. He will not let it go unless that person repents. On the other hand, you will not be able to heal, move on, and, in particular, help rescue your child or loved one if you do not release it to the King of Kings. And by doing that, you will be freed to operate in the authority God intends for you to walk in.

Let me give you a true-life example. Hannah, one of my friends, was cheated on by her then-husband and left with a one-year-old. She was brokenhearted at the thought of letting her daughter have visitation with her ex and the ungodly woman with whom he had cheated. Hannah wanted to protect her daughter from that lady. Hannah knew she had to forgive or release them to move on, heal, and regain her life. Her feelings were of hurt, anger, and betrayal. *But she trusted God and His Word more than her feelings.* Hannah told me that she was curled up on the bed, crying out to God, feeling like it would be easier if He would just take her on to heaven than to forgive them. She made herself say the words, even though the feelings were not there. Remember, feelings are fickle and can deceive you. You release them and ask the Holy Spirit to remove those negative feelings. Again, you are not saying that what they did was right. *You are releasing them so that you can move on and that God can move for you.* Almost immediately, the miracle happened. The day after she forgave them, she got a call from her ex-husband telling her he and that lady had broken up. When we get out of the driver's or judgment seat, we untie God's hands to move on our behalf. Brad and I had to forgive the girl stalking him almost daily. It was by an act of our will. Choose this day whom you will serve. We chose to keep it where God could move on our behalf!

Some of you are stuck in unforgiveness against yourselves. Understand that any unforgiveness will hinder you in your pursuit of winning back the lives of those you love. Many years ago, I had a vivid God dream where I walked into where a lady was sleeping. I started beating the literal hell out of her. I am not a violent person in real life at all, so this dream shook me. I kept hitting her over and over again. When I finally stopped, I looked at this lady. It was crazy. At first, I only recognized that she looked vaguely familiar. But then, as I looked past her bloody and bruised face and body and looked at her eyes. I was shocked. It was me, except an extremely malnourished, abused, broken version of myself. I asked the Holy Spirit to show me what that was about. I heard softly in my heart, "Kerry, I forgave you as soon as you asked for forgiveness. What you are seeing is your spirit man. You have not forgiven yourself. And not only have you not forgiven yourself, but you bring it back up and batter yourself with it." Ugh! He told me to start speaking to myself and treating myself with the same love I spoke to and treated my children. I repented for my behavior. God does not motivate you by talking down to you or beating you up. Period! He is a merciful, loving God.

Another area of bitterness and unforgiveness that needs to be addressed is your relationship with God. Some of you blame God for something bad that happened in your life. God has no sin and is love. So understand that your judgment of God is misplaced. He is not your enemy. You may understand this in your head, but still, you may feel that He let you down in one way or another. You may feel that He did not live up to the expectations that you set. He loves you so very much and wants only good for you. He is a good and loving Father. You live in a fallen world with an enemy who is literally out to destroy you. Trusting in God, even when it is out of the boundaries of reasoning, is imperative. Humble yourself before God and ask forgiveness. You must trust God to operate fully in the authority that he has given to you. Feelings are fickle and can play tricks on you, but God is constant. He never changes and will uphold you through the entire process.

I know it is hard to understand. But unforgiveness and bitterness are like roots that grow up and surround your hands and feet. It fills your mind, will, and emotions so that you are locked down and powerless to be who God called you to be. Some of you are holding unforgiveness towards God. It is time to take that power back. God wants you healed, whole, and free. He wants your loved ones healed, whole, and free also! God loves you!

———————— ⚔️ ————————

Prayer of Release from Unforgiveness and Bitterness:

Dear Lord, I come before You now, and my love for You and my child is greater than the feelings of hate. I choose by an act of my will to forgive _____. I choose by an act of my will to forgive myself and You where I have held unforgiveness. I choose by an act of my will to release

those I have held in judgment. I ask You, Holy Spirit, to take the negative feelings away. I ask You to pull up all unforgiveness and bitterness from the roots. I desire to fully walk in the authority that You died for, and I choose to lay down all rights to punish the person who has harmed me at the feet of Jesus. I choose to trust you, Lord, because your Word says to *trust in the Lord with all thine heart; and lean not untomy own understanding. In all my ways, acknowledge him, and he shall direct my paths* (*see* Proverbs 3:5-6).

In Jesus's Name I pray,

Amen.

Chapter Seven

The Action that Produces the Reaction

What is your primary motive for wanting to reach or rescue the person? If it is born out of a desire for revenge or self-servitude, then you completely miss the point. If we do it without love, then the fruit of it will rot. Love is the key and should be the motivating factor that drives us. We should pray to have our heart posture to represent God's heart for the lost. And if we are not rooted and grounded in love, then we will not affect the atmosphere with the glory of God. The Glory or presence of God will quicken the lost and draw them back to Him. It is His Presence that will destroy the yoke that has been placed on our loved ones. Isaiah 10:27, "It shall come to pass in that day that his burden will be taken away from your shoulder, And his yoke from your neck, And the yoke will be destroyed because of the anointing oil."

Not only must you walk in forgiveness with people, but your love walk is an essential key to operating in the authority necessary to rescue your children and the other lost souls. Remember, in Psalm 23, He tells us that He will "restore our soul," which is our mind, will, and emotions. He restores our souls and fills us so full that we overflow with that abundance of love so that we can pour out on our families and the lost to produce change.

While at a morning prayer meeting, I noticed a young Bible school student who looked to be from another country crying with his hands raised. I immediately felt such compassion for him, thinking that it must be very hard being away from his home. I heard the Holy Spirit tell me, "Kerry, go give him a 'momma' hug." At that moment, I was overwhelmed with such compassion and empathy for him, and I just wanted him to know that God loved him. I did what God had led me to do, and while hugging him, that young man bent over and was delivered from a demonic bondage that was holding him captive. Remember, the anointing destroys the yoke! It destroys it. I think it surprised both him and me. Out of God's love, miracles happen. I challenge you to get so full of God and set your faith on the fact that when you go into the spiritual and physical places where familiar spirits are, you bring the overflowing, yoke-destroying, Holy Spirit-charged love of God with you in abundance.

Corinthians 13:1-8

Though I speak with the tongues of men and of angels, but have not love, I have become sounding brass or a clanging cymbal. And though I have the gift of prophecy, and understand all mysteries and all knowledge, and though I have all faith, so that I could remove mountains, but have not love, I am nothing. And though I bestow all my goods to feed the poor, and though I give my body to be burned, but have not love, it profits me nothing. Love suffers long and is kind; love does not envy; love does not parade itself, is not puffed up; does not behave rudely, does not seek its own, is not provoked, thinks no evil; does not rejoice in iniquity, but rejoices in the truth; bears all things, believes all things, hopes all things, endures all things. Love never fails.

Chapter Eight

Understanding Your Authority and the Power of the Blood

What are we to do when faced with our loved ones being caught in the most cunning of nets and understanding that in ourselves, we can do nothing? Many of us have tried all we know to help them. But for the Grace of God, they will forever be stuck because we cannot of ourselves rescue them. But with God, He gives us a way of escape! The Spirit of God will not only intercede for us, but He will also intervene for us! Remember, "all things are possible to him who believes" (Mark 9:23).

We are told to put on the whole armor of God. In Ephesians 6:9-13, we read: "Finally, my brethren, be strong in the Lord and in the power of His might. Put on the whole armor of God, that you may be able to stand against the wiles of the devil. For we do not wrestle against flesh and blood, but against principalities, against powers, against the rulers of the darkness of this age, against spiritual hosts of wickedness in the heavenly places. Therefore take up the whole armor of God, that you may be able to withstand in the evil day, and having done all, to stand." Why would God tell us in His Word to put on the armor if we are going to do nothing with it but sit and cry in our houses about how the enemy came and stole our children? What is it that you are believing in God for? If it is in line with God's promises, you need to get out of your pity party state, remember who you are in Christ, and start acting like a child of God! "Now faith is the assurance of things hoped for, the conviction of things not seen" (Hebrews 11:1). Faith trusts who God is and what He says in His Word!

How do we deal with the arrows that are flying toward us daily? We hit them with the Word of God as He tells us in Ephesians:6-7, "above all, taking the shield of faith with which you will be able to quench all the fiery darts of the wicked one. And take the helmet of salvation and the sword of the Spirit, which is the word of God." Look in Acts 28, when Paul went to the island of Malta. He had a poisonous snake bite him. Everyone is sitting around waiting for him to die. He just shook it off his hand and kept on moving with no long-term effects of harm. That same power is available to you. You will get through this mess and look back and see the miracle of God like my family did. The Bible says in Romans 8:11, "But if the

Spirit of Him who raised Jesus from the dead dwells in you, He who raised Christ from the dead will also give life to your mortal bodies through His Spirit who dwells in you."

By what right do we, as God's children, have to operate in His authority? In Luke 10:19, the Word says, " Behold, I give you the authority to trample on serpents and scorpions, and over all the power of the enemy, and nothing shall by any means hurt you." In Romans 5:17, we see that "For if by the one man's offense (Adam) death reigned through the one, much more those who receive abundance of grace and of the gift of righteousness will reign in life through the One, Jesus Christ." Do you see that? It says we will reign IN LIFE. The *Amplified Classic* says we will reign "AS KINGS IN LIFE."[5] We have been transferred to God's kingdom when we accepted Jesus as our Savior. "He has delivered us from the power of darkness and conveyed (*transferred*) us into the kingdom of the Son of His love" (Colossians 1:13). Lastly, we are to take the authority over the enemy and rule and reign as kings and priests. "To Him who loved us and washed us from our sins in His own blood, and has made us kings and priests to His God and Father, to Him be glory and dominion forever and ever. Amen" (Revelations 1:5-6).

Do you want to know how salvation for yourself, your children, and the lost will come? It will come through the blood of Jesus. Satan sits before the throne of God, accusing us and accusing our children. And let us be clear: in truth, you, your child, or your loved one may have committed the accused sin. Understand that having your children stolen is under the curse mentioned in

Deuteronomy 28:32, "Your sons and your daughters shall be given to another people, and your eyes shall look and fail with longing for them all day long." But for the blood of Jesus, we would have no recourse. But because He was the blameless, sinless sacrifice and took our place, we have been saved from that curse. The blood of Jesus is our legal right to stand and petition our Father God for mercy and justice in this case. That is why we "plead the blood of Jesus" over our situation and those who need rescuing. It is like in a courtroom when asked, "How do you plead guilty or not guilty?" We plead, "the blood of Jesus!"

Galatians 3:13-14

Christ has redeemed us from the curse of the law, having become a curse for us (for it is written, "Cursed is everyone who hangs on a tree"), that the blessing of Abraham might come upon the Gentiles in Christ Jesus, that we might receive the promise of the Spirit through faith.

Revelation 12:10-11

Then I heard a loud voice saying in heaven, 'Now salvation, and strength, and the kingdom of our God, and the power of His Christ have come, for the accuser of our brethren, who accused them before our God day and night, has been cast down. And they overcame him by the blood of the Lamb and by the word of their testimony, and they did not love their lives to the death.

When I was 19 years old, I went with my college roommates Shannon and Charlotte to Shannon's hometown of

Chicago. She wanted to show us the city reflecting on the water at night. Being young and small-town girls, Charlotte and I had no concept of the dangers that could be out there. Plus, we had a couple of Shannon's guy friends with us, so we felt safe. Once there, the big high-rises and all the lights reflecting off of Lake Michigan water were mesmerizing. I was so taken by the beauty that I wasn't aware of what was happening. I heard my friend Shannon say my name, but it sounded like it was from a distance. I turned and looked, and she, Charlotte, and the two guys were 30 feet from me, headed toward their car. Shannon was saying, "Kerry, Kerry, come on!" I did not understand why we were leaving so quickly, but then I looked to the left and saw what looked like a gang getting out of a couple of vehicles. They were hooping and hollering while walking toward us and saying things like "fresh meat." Now, as an adult, as I look back, it was an extremely dangerous situation. We had to walk right in front of these men to get safely to the car.

Growing up, Momma had taught me about the power of the blood of Jesus. She had always "pled the blood of Jesus" over me and my siblings. So immediately, it sprang up out of my mouth. I started yelling, "I plead the blood of Jesus, I plead the blood, I draw a bloodline, I bind you up now in the Name of Jesus." Then, I prayed in tongues and kept moving. At that moment, an amazing thing happened, and it has marked my life with the power found in the blood when we use it with authority. It was like all these men hit a wall. They went up to a point, and they did not come further. I could walk past them to the car, and they could not move closer. I am convinced that they hit a wall of angels. We were able to leave safely. This situation was an example of a direct demonic assignment sent, but how the blood of Jesus covered and protected us through it. Start pleading the blood over yourself, your children, and the lost. There is such power in the blood of Jesus!

God tells us we are "more than conquerors" in Christ Jesus! (Romans 8:37). Trust Jesus and walk in the authority He gives you. He tells us that "whatever you bind on earth will be bound in heaven, and whatever you loose on earth will be loosed in heaven" (Matthew 18:18). Jesus gives us "power of attorney" using His Name! How awesome is that! He says in John 14:13-14, "and whatever you ask in My name, that I will do, that the Father may be glorified in the Son. If you ask anything in My name, I will do it."

I know many people get stuck here. It is like you saying to your daddy, "Dad, I need to go to the store." He smiled and said, "Okay, here are the keys. You can take my car." But instead of taking the car, you sit there and cry that you are stuck at home and not at the store. The vehicle to get there has been provided. The key to start the car was given to you. It is now your job to go! You may say, "Kerry, I am in the car, ready to get them. But I do not know how." Do not fear! I'll give you what worked for us, and God will not leave you without an answer. Remember that God tells us, "It is the glory of God to conceal a matter, But the glory of kings is to search out a matter" (Proverbs 25:2). Have faith in God that the key to rescuing your people will be revealed to you! He is a loving, faithful, and just God. Failure would be for you to settle for a condition that you know in your heart is not right and is contrary to God's Word! Do not give up because it seems complicated! God has given you the power and authority. Now, it is time for you to walk in it!

Jeremiah 31:16-17

Thus says the Lord: "Refrain your voice from weeping, And your eyes from tears; For your work shall be rewarded, says the Lord, And they shall come back from the land of the enemy. There is hope in your future, says the Lord, That your children shall come back to their own border.

Declaration of Faith to Take Your Place of Authority
Based on Isaiah 61, Job 11:5, 1 Peter 4

(I say this over myself, my husband, my boys, and their wives daily.)

The Spirit of the Lord is on me and _____, and the Lord has anointed and qualified us to preach the Gospel of good tidings to the meek, the poor, and the afflicted. He has sent us to bind up and heal the brokenhearted, to proclaim liberty to the captives, and open the prison of those who are bound. We are all oaks of righteousness. We are priests of the Lord and ministers of God. We are steadfast and secure. We are well-balanced and cautious. We are firmly rooted, established, strong, immovable, determined, grounded securely, and strengthened by God.

In Jesus's Name I pray,

Amen.

Chapter Nine

What's in Your Words?

Part of operating in your God-given authority is under-standing that your words have the power to take flight and do what they were sent to do. They also have the power to cancel everything you are standing for. In your words is the power to decree, also known as confess, what God says over a matter. You decree it, and then God establishes it! You also can cancel your prayers and petitions by negative talk. "For by your words you will be justified, and by your words, you will be condemned" (Matthew 12:37). We must watch over the words that we let come out of our mouths! "Set a guard, O LORD, over my mouth; Keep watch over the door of my lips" (Psalm 141:3).

Let us put this in a practical scenario. Let's say you are in a courtroom, and your accuser can use your very own words against you. "Judge, I know that Barbara is standing for her daughter, but she herself calls her a liar and a thief. She herself said her daughter is "a lazy, good-for-nothing, and messed up, crazy human being." Do you see how that would look? You must watch your words because, as we saw earlier, your words can move mountains, but they can also condemn you. Death and life are in the power of the tongue, And those who love it will eat its fruit (Proverbs 18:21). Okay, let's look at this same courtroom situation, but from the perspective of a momma who has been guarding her mouth and what she says. Barbara's words testify this before the Judge, "I plead the blood of Jesus over my daughter. I thank God that she is a blood-bought child of God. I thank you that no weapon formed against her shall prosper. I thank you that her eyes are open and that she sees that You are the One true God. I thank you that my daughter's loving, kind, respectful, humble, and gentle. I thank You that she walks in the wisdom of God."

In the same way that you should guard your mouth when standing for healing. You must guard your mouth when speaking of the one you want to save or help. When my son, Brandon, was going through his cancer battle, we were going to the doctors and hearing the diagnosis. The diagnosis was the facts. But despite the diagnosis, we knew and clung to what God said about it over what we were hearing. I look at it like this: the FACTS of the case or situation versus the TRUTH of the case. And the TRUTH, which is Jesus, the Word of God, is a higher authority and higher power. THE FACTS OF THE CASE MUST BOW THEIR KNEE TO THE TRUTH.

Okay, now here is an important nugget. You've heard it said in Matthew 7:6, "Do not give what is holy to the dogs; nor cast your pearls before swine, lest they trample them under their feet, and turn and tear you in pieces." Do not go and tell everybody your business because not everyone will guard their mouths when speaking about your child, yourself, or the situation. In truth, it is not wise to do. Confide with those who can join arms with you in faith. Tell those who will speak life into the situation. Tell those who will help hold your arms up when you are tired and will surround you with prayer. I had a pretty small circle who really knew the details of our day-to-day situations. But my Jesus knew it all!!!

When I was young, I would just tell everybody all of my business. I was a "never meet a stranger" person, but in my naivety, I opened myself up to some vicious attacks. I truly believed that everyone had good intentions for everyone else. My sister, Jenny, helped teach me not to let strangers or new acquaintances into the "bedroom" or intimate details of my life. I learned how to keep some people on the front porch, some I would allow in the living room, and only my closest friends in the bedroom of my life. The bedroom friends had earned the right to help "guard" the intimate details of my life. This is the case when sharing details of your situation with others. Be vague but positive when "living room" friends ask, "How is John doing?" The answer is, "He is doing good, facing a few challenges, but he's an overcomer and will get through it." Then, do not get into any more details. Guard your mouth! When we had people, even relatives, throw out words over Brandon and Brad that were contrary to God's Word, I would just pull those words down. Often, just under my breath, in a whisper, I would pull those words down and replace them with TRUTH.

Go to the Word and search for God's promises. We bring things from the spiritual realm into the natural realm by speaking God's Word out loud. We do our part and trust the Holy Spirit to do His! We put faith over fear by guarding our mouths and refusing to speak things contrary to what the Word of God says about our situation. And if you mess up now and then, just quickly repent, pull those words down, and replace them with the TRUTH!

Prayer to Reverse Negative Words Spoken:

LORD, by the power of the Blood and in the authority of Jesus Name, I ask forgiveness and pull down every negative word that I have spoken over myself, my family, and in particular _____.
I ask forgiveness where I have spoken not in a loving way or where I have spoken contrary to what God's Word says. Please reveal to me, by your Spirit, every word curse set against me and _____. I bind up every spell, curse, voodoo curse, or incantation set against me, my family and _____. I renounce them now in the name of Jesus. I loose the power of

God and ask the angels to go on our behalf and pull them down. I thank you, Lord.

In Jesus's Name I pray,

Amen.

Chapter Ten

Action Steps: Let's Go!

We all have people we love or whom God has placed in our circles who need Jesus or to be set free from a situation. God gives us specific weapons for us to use. We know the goal: to reach, rescue, and ultimately get people delivered and set free from the snares set for them. But how specifically? When we were searching for answers, I wanted to find them in the Word of God. I know and trust the Word has all the answers, but finding those answers can sometimes be a process. My family and I prayed in the spirit and asked for God's wisdom. While at a prayer meeting I regularly attend, one of the leaders shared with us a Dutch Sheets: Give Him 15 message about rescuing the lost.[2] I listened and thought, "Wait, what?" Is this true? I've been a Christian for over 50 years but had never heard this scripture used in this application. It gave me hope that there was more that we could do than just pray for laborers to come into their path and for their eyes to be opened. It gave a strategic plan. God shows us how to go after our people in the Spirit proactively! For the first time, this was getting exciting. Hope is a beautiful thing, and I now have it! God is so faithful.

Depending on the "camp, stream, or denomination" you are in, you may or may not have known this. Try not to shut it out because you have a preconceived notion of what I am about to share. Instead, I strongly encourage you, as I did, to research the Hebrew/Greek meanings of these words and the context to whom it is spoken. In 2 Corinthians 10:4-6, the Bible tells us, "For the weapons of our warfare are not carnal but mighty in God for pulling down strongholds, casting down arguments and every high thing that exalts itself against the knowledge of God, bringing every thought into captivity to the obedience of Christ, and being ready to punish all disobedience when your obedience is fulfilled."

In my circle, and I believe correctly, I was taught that we use this scripture to pull down the strongholds built in our minds. I had not heard that we could also use this scripture to go after negative strongholds in other people's minds as a weapon of war! This insight is amazing! My husband pointed out, "Yes, it is like any competitor knows, you must have the correct mindset first, and then you can go after your competitor. It is like when you play a tennis match. You have an opponent that you must come against, but you also have to pull down your own negative thoughts of fear, inadequacies, and defeatism to defeat your opponent." Such a great example!

Let us look at the Strong's Concordance to verify what we have heard:

- **Weapons** 3696 *hóplon*: an implement or utensil or tool (literally or figuratively, especially, offensive for war): armour, instrument, weapon
- **Warfare** 4752 *strateia*: military service, warfare
- **Pulling down** 2506 *kathaíresis*-demolition; figuratively, extinction: destruction, pulling down
- **Strongholds** 3794 *ochuróma*: a castle (figuratively, argument): stronghold
- **Casting down** 2507 *kathaireó*: to lower (or with violence) demolish (literally or figuratively): cast (pull, put, take) down, destroy
- **Arguments** 3053 *logismos*: reasoning (conscience, conceit): imagination, thought
- **Captivity** 163 *aichmalótizó*: to make captive: lead away captive, bring into captivity
- **Punish** 1556. *Ekdikeó* to vindicate, retaliate, punish: a (re-)venge
- **Fulfilled** 4137 *Pleroo* to make replete, satisfy, execute (an office), finish (a period or task), verify (or coincide with a prediction), etc.: accomplish, X after, (be) complete, end, expire, fill (up), fulfill, (be, make) full (come), fully preach, perfect, supply[3]

All of these show our ability to use these weapons to get justice for our children and the lost. But only after we have first dealt with all unforgiveness and sin in our own lives. (2 Cor. 10:6: "being ready to punish all disobedience when your obedience is fulfilled.") In other words, once we have taken the "log" out of our eyes, we can be ready to help others! "Or how can you say to your brother, 'Let me remove the speck from your eye'; and look, a plank is in your own eye? Hypocrite! First, remove the plank from your own eye, and then you will see clearly to remove the speck from your brother's eye" (Matthew 7:4-5).

In the context of 2 Corinthians 10:4-6, Paul was challenged by false teachers in the Corinthian church who were questioning his authority. He understood that "we do not wrestle against flesh and blood, but against principalities, against powers, against the rulers of the darkness of this age, against spiritual hosts of wickedness in the heavenly places." In other words, he understood the bigger picture, like we need to do. As children of God, we cannot expect to win spiritual battles with human force. We must pray in the spirit and our understanding and speak God's Word by faith to see those mountains move in our lives! Hebrews 4:12 says, "For the word of God is living and powerful, and sharper than any two-edged sword, piercing even to the division of soul and spirit, and of joints and marrow, and is a discerner of the thoughts and intents of the heart."

Let us break down specifically how 2 Corinthians is showing us to apply the authority given to us by God. This scripture tells us how to use these weapons, which is the authority of the believer, in order to actively pull down and destroy the deceptive thoughts, arguments, and pride that have kept people in bondage. Just as we know that "faith without works is dead," so is authority without action. Most of us just pray the Ephesians prayer over them, "Lord, open their eyes, that they may see the hope of your calling"(Eph.1:18-21), which is an excellent prayer. Or we pray for laborers to be sent in their paths (Matthew 9:38). Perfect! But we should not stop there! What if we were given specific weapons to use, and we were not using them? It is like someone caught in a net, and we are trying to untwist them. God has given us scissors to cut through that entanglement, but we are ignorant of them or are so focused on our way that we do not see the tools that God has provided for us. PRISONERS, CAPTIVES, SLAVES need someone to open the prison doors. They need someone to help them. God has given us keys in His Word, and we can actively use God's authority, in His Name and by His Blood, to open the doors!

Christ was sent to proclaim "release to the captives." "The Spirit of the Lord is upon Me, because He has anointed me to preach the gospel to the poor; He has sent me to heal the brokenhearted, to proclaim liberty to the captives and recovery of sight to the blind, to set at liberty those who are oppressed; to proclaim the acceptable year of the Lord" (Luke 4:18-19). In light of the 2 Corinthians 10:4-6 scripture, the three major components that need to be addressed are arguments, pride, and thoughts. Seek God in prayer and ask Him to reveal the specific stronghold that the person or people you are standing for are dealing with. Ask Him, pray in the Spirit, and then listen.

Prayer to Reveal Strongholds

Dear Lord,

I thank You, God, that You are a waymaker and that You bring hidden things into the light. I come boldly before Your throne of grace now and ask that all strongholds that are causing a hindrance and blindness to _____ be revealed. I thank you in advance and take it by faith.

In Jesus's Name I pray,

Amen.

(Now, take time to listen to what the Holy Spirit says. Also, if you are able to be around this person, listen. Frequently, people will speak it in their own words.)

Chapter Eleven

Prophesy
to the Breath!

Not long ago, I was in prayer for my family. "Lord, is there yet more we can do? I have done all I know to go after my lost loved ones, and I have so many friends who have children who have walked away from their faith and are in some pretty ungodly situations. Show us Your plan, Lord. I trust You and know that You did not leave us without hope. You have saved my sons, and I am extremely grateful. Yet, there are more still that need to find you. They have been deceived, hurt, abandoned, lied to, and hit with horrible blows. Some have never known you; others have fallen away because of Satan's demonic assignments. Please show us Your ways, Lord. You are a loving God and a merciful Father. I know You have a way of escape. Please reveal it to us." As I prayed this, the Holy Spirit led me to read Ezekiel 37. I read it, and He kept bringing it back to me. So I sat on it for a while and listened to Him. He told me to reread it. I started reading the following, and this is what happened.

Ezekiel 37:1-8

The hand of the LORD came upon me and brought me out in the Spirit of the LORD, and set me down in the midst of the valley; and it was full of bones. Then He caused me to pass by them all around, and behold, there were very many in the open valley; and indeed they were very dry. And He said to me, "Son of man, can these bones live?" So I answered, "O Lord GOD, You know.

Again He said to me, "Prophesy to these bones, and say to them, 'O dry bones, hear the word of the LORD! Thus says the Lord GOD to these bones: "Surely I will cause breath to enter into you, and you shall live. I will put sinews on you and bring flesh upon you, cover you with skin and put breath in you; and you shall live. Then you shall know that I am the LORD." '" (*The Amplified Classic* says that "you shall know, understand, and realize that I am the Lord.")[5]

So I prophesied as I was commanded; and as I prophesied, there was a noise, and suddenly a rattling; and the bones came together, bone to bone. Indeed, as I looked, the sinews and the flesh came upon them, and the skin covered them over; but there was no breath in them.

He stopped me here and asked me a question. "What do you have here?" I read it and thought about the miracle that they had gotten all their muscles and skin on them again. But as I looked closer, I said. "Lord, it is just a bunch of dead bodies." "Correct," He said. Oftentimes, you hear it taught to prophesy or speak to the dry bones to live. But even after Ezekiel did that, they were still not functioning. They were still dead. *Here is where many people give up right in the middle of their miracle.* The Word had already been spoken for them to live. Take note that at that moment, they were still just a pile of dead bodies in the natural realm. Some of you have children or people who need to be called back to the land of the living. I know I do! Remember, just like the Lord had Ezekiel do, we first need to prophesy to the dry bones to live, BUT THEN need to prophesy to the breath to come from the four winds of the Holy Spirit to quicken them!

Ezekiel 37:9-10

Also He said to me, "Prophesy to the breath, prophesy, son of man, and say to the breath, 'Thus says the Lord God: "Come from the four winds, O breath, and breathe on these slain, that they may live." ' " So I prophesied as He commanded me, and breath came into them, and they lived, and stood upon their feet, an exceedingly great army.

I heard the Holy Spirit say, "Kerry, I want you to pray this over every dead thing in your life. List them out. Everything and everybody you can think of that needs resurrection life called back into it. But most importantly, call it over the lost sheep, the prodigals, the stalked, and the trapped. Run after them with all diligence. The same words I told Ezekiel to say, I want you to speak this over them. Do not stop there. Speak it over all of my children, My beloved. Use the power I gave you and speak it into existence."

So, I started making a list, and the list is long. I realized that we have gotten used to living with death: Dead relationships, dead dreams, dead bank accounts, dead hopes, dead businesses, death. And death is not meant to be lived with. It stinks and attracts disease, rats, hopelessness, and darkness. It is the opposite of what Jesus paid the ultimate price for. He died so we "may have life" and that we "may have it more abundantly" (John 10:10).

I started looking up the "four winds" in this scripture. It is referenced nine different times in the Bible. I found that In 1890, Charles H. Spurgeon, a minister who had won thousands upon thousands of souls for Christ, used Ezekiel 37:1-10 to evangelize people. In hindsight, seeing the fruit of his labor, I feel confident that it is a solid scripture on which we can stand!

In his sermon entitled, "Come from the Four Winds, O Breath!" from May 15th, 1890, Spurgeon referenced the dry bones scripture. He says that there are many interpretations of this text, that the Word is multifaceted, and that we are to, in essence, gleam from it what we can. I love that God is so much bigger than us and hides jewels in his Word for those willing to search them out. That is one of the beautiful things about the Holy Spirit. He speaks life to us through God's word.[4]

Spurgeon acknowledges that there are many theological thoughts about Ezekiel 37. He says that some people see a story of the resurrection of the dead after the trumpet sounds, some think it refers to three types of res-urrections, and some think this scripture refers to the host of Israel. But Spurgeon used this scripture to go after the lost, and with the track record of souls won, it bears much weight! In this sermon, he states, "There are others who, looking beyond the literal for the spiritual teaching, see, and I think, rightly see, that here is a picture of the recovery of ungodly men from their spiritual death and corruption — a parable of how sinners are brought up from their hopeless, spiritually dead condition, and made to live by the power of the Holy Ghost."[4]

God gives us practical ways to use his scriptures. We want to rescue our loved ones and other lost souls. God shows us, specifically here, how to do it. We need our children, family, friends, and the lost as a whole to come back from the land of the dead, like what happened when Ezekiel prophesied for the bones to live and the breath and wind to blow. All the things needed for that to happen came together. The uniting structures, systems, muscles, and ligaments needed to bind it together and give it strength came together. We need this for our people. The sinew reconnects the dead to their purpose! The skin provides a layer of protection, and we get that by pleading the Blood of Jesus over our people. In Ezekiel 37:6, the Word says, "You shall know, understand, and realize that I am the Lord." Our goal is for those that we are praying for to know, understand, and realize that Jesus is the only way by way of the cross. We want the "eyes of their understanding to be enlightened," as we find in Ephesians 1:18.

You may say, "I have shared about Jesus and his redemption, and I have hit a brick wall. They don't want to hear from me or have anything to do with me." Deception is such a wicked thing, but fear not! Spurgeon himself speaks of this saying, "We come all of a sudden upon an iron-bound coast and can get no further. We find that men are dead; what is wanted is that they shall be quickened, and *we* cannot quicken them."[4] But the Holy Spirit can! Jesus understands your heart cry, broken-hearted and frustrated over the current circumstances. Fear not! We are not like those without hope! God gives us keys. And calling to the dead bones to live and calling the breath and life to come back into them is one of the keys that God provides us.

As believers and co-laborers of Christ, we can use methods to reach our loved ones. Let us stay confident that we will see the salvation of our Lord! As a family, the Holy Spirit led us in rescuing our sons, and He will lead you, too. I still have lost deceived, hurting, and trapped family members. I fully intend to see each of them have a relationship with Christ. God is so faithful. Remember, as a "co-laborer" with Christ, we do our part. We do the praying, staying in faith, watching our words, staying in forgiveness, following the Holy Spirit's leading, walking in love, professing, declaring, and prophesying part. It is the Spirit of God that *can* and *will* give life to them. Zechariah 4:6 says, "Not by might nor by power, but by My Spirit,' says the Lord of hosts." He gives the life. He is Life! We must stay in faith!

Chapter Twelve

Prayer and Declarations of Faith for Rescuing the Lost Prodigals, Stalked, and Ensnared

In our times, we are surrounded by voices of hopelessness. But it is not right, nor is it Biblically based, to be hopeless. In Proverbs 13:12, we see that "hope deferred makes the heart sick." Many times, it is a demonic spirit that needs to be addressed. People entertain the demonic and think that they are enduring for Christ. Remember that hopelessness is a place of being void of the breakthrough power of our God. We, at times, entertain those voices that strip us of hope for our situation. God designed you to carry hope for every circumstance. I cannot say this loud enough: *in every situation, there is a way for God to show up and show out!* He loves us so very much and is the God of the breakthrough. Biblical hope is different than any old hope because it is *absolute*. The God of the breakthrough said it in His Word, you believe it, and that settles it. I am praying this over you and coming into agreement with you that the demonic oppression of hopelessness is broken over your life right now.

> **"Lord, I come before you now in the name of Jesus and by the power of His blood representing those hearing this and wanting help rescuing their loved ones, the ensnared, trapped, stalked and lost. I break all hopelessness from speaking in their lives. It is an illegal assignment, and I bind it up now and command it to stop speaking to them now. I ask that you give each person a revelation of the power of hope in their lives. In Jesus's Name, I pray, Amen."**

As believers and co-laborers of Christ, we have a good shepherd. He has given us the rescue plan. It is our responsibility to do our part. We are "co-laborers" with Him. Let us stay confident that we will see the salvation of our Lord! As a family, the Holy Spirit led us in rescuing our sons, and He will lead you, too. My oldest is healed and whole and is married to his love, Emily. My youngest is set free from both traps set to enslave him, completely restored, and married to his love, Julia. Yet even in these victories, I stay vigilant. God has called us to be watchmen on the wall. God is so faithful. Remember, as "co-laborer" with Christ, we do our part. We do the praying, staying in faith, watching our words, staying in forgiveness, following the Holy Spirit's leading, walking in love, professing, declaring, and prophesying part. It is the Spirit of God that can and will give life to them. Zechariah 4:6 says, "Not by might nor by power, but by My Spirit, says the Lord of hosts." He gives the life. He is Life! It is the anointing that destroys the yokes! (*see* Isaiah 10:27) We must stay in faith!

Prayer and intercession must be at the core of recovering the lost children to God and separating them from the demonic assignments. Walking in God's love and forgiveness while uprooting all bitterness will allow you the freedom to move in the power and authority needed to rescue your loved ones. Another key is standing on God's Word and using it in professions and declarations of faith. Understand that the reason why this happened is a strategic hit on you and your family. Trust that God has provided us with strategic ways to combat the attack. Understand and use the authority God gave to His children, and go after those in your sphere of influence to reach with all diligence. Spiritual warfare is not for the faint at heart, but I stand with you, believing that we will see the salvation of our God! Now go get your people!

Prayer and Confession to Rescue the Lost, Stalked, and Prodigals

In the name of the Lord Jesus Christ and by the power of His blood, I am using the authority given to me in 2 Corinthians 10:4-6.

I stand, interceding for the following: (Name of those you are standing for) _____

_____

_____

_____I am destroying all strongholds set, including _____, religion, hurt, abuse, witchcraft, manipulation, control, rejection, addiction, fornication, unholiness, unforgiveness, pride, abandonment, deceit, lust, anger, cursing, pornography, depression, suicide, lack, confusion, hopelessness, and command all demonic assignments to stop and desist in their life.

These weapons given to me by God (2 Cor. 10:4-6) can break down every proud argument against God and every wall that can be built that keeps men from finding Him. I tear it down now, in the Name of Jesus! With these weapons and God's authority, I can capture rebels and bring them back to God. I decree that their heart's desire is obedience to Christ. I decree that they are set free from pride and rebellion, and their heart belongs to God.

No weapon formed against them shall prosper. I bind your plans, Satan, in the authority of Jesus's Name and by His blood. I take every thought, plan, temptation, allurement, scheme, and demonic assignment captive. I ask the Lord to send laborers in their paths. I ask for the eyes of their understanding to be enlightened so that they would know the hope of your calling. I ask for the anointing to go now and destroy the yoke and cords set upon them. I decree, in the name of Jesus and by His blood, THAT IT IS DONE.

Hear the Word of the Lord today! Oh, you dry bones. Behold, the Lord will cause breath and spirit to enter you, and you shall live! (This is my proclamation of Faith!)

And He will lay sinews upon you (reconnecting you to your purpose.)

He will bring flesh upon you and cover you with skin. (This is His hedge of protection!)

He will put breath and spirit in you, and you shall live! (And declare the works of the Lord!)

I decree what God says in His Word, that (a.) you shall know, (b.) understand, (c.)and realize that He is the Lord! (Ezekiel 37:6 AMPC)[5]

Thus says the Lord God: Come from the four winds, O breath, and spirit, and breathe upon these slain that they may live (Get up out of that grave!) And stand up on your feet, an exceedingly great army!

(Holy Spirit, breathe on them Your resurrection life!) But if the Spirit of Him who raised Jesus from the dead dwells in you, He who raised Christ from the dead will also give life to your mortal bodies through His Spirit who dwells in you. (Romans 8:11-13)

In Jesus's Name, I pray,

Amen.

Prayer and Declarations are based on these scriptures:

2 Corinthians 10:4-6

For the weapons of our warfare are not carnal but mighty in God for pulling down strongholds, casting down arguments and every high thing that exalts itself against the knowledge of God, bringing every thought into captivity to the obedience of Christ, and being ready to punish all disobedience when your obedience is fulfilled.

Ezekial 37:1-10

Again He said to me, "Prophesy to these bones, and say to them, 'O dry bones, hear the word of the Lord! Thus says the Lord God to these bones: "Surely I will cause breath to enter into you, and you shall live. I will put sinews on you and bring flesh upon you, cover you with skin and put breath in you; and you shall live. Then you shall know that I am the Lord."' "So I prophesied as I was commanded; and as I prophesied, there was a noise, and suddenly a rattling; and the bones came together, bone to bone.

Indeed, as I looked, the sinews and the flesh came upon them, and the skin covered them over; but there was no breath in them. Also, He said to me, "Prophesy to the breath, prophesy, son of man, and say to the breath, 'Thus says the Lord God: "Come from the four winds, O breath, and breathe on these slain, that they may live." ' " So I prophesied as He commanded me, and breath came into them, and they lived, and stood upon their feet, an exceedingly great army."

A Special Note for those Praying for Prodigals

One final thought: as your sons, daughters, spouses, grandchildren, nieces, and nephews return. Help them to re-enter without shame. I had a dream about one of my nieces that is not living for the Lord right now. I saw her awkwardly crunched down underneath a folding chair. She wore clothing that was more in line with a middle school girl and had her hair in two ponytails. I noticed she was embarrassed but did not know how to get out of this situation. In the dream, I started helping her to get out of that trap while not trying to let others see her. When I woke up, my heart had such compassion for her. Who among us has not been in the same situation? God's heart is to help us all reconcile to who He created us to be without the shame of a scarlet letter to be worn by us. Jesus paid the price so that we do not have to. "…But love covers all sins." (Proverbs 10:12)

Take, for example, the original prodigal son. He asked for his inheritance, took it, and squandered it on harlots and partying. He found himself in a pig pen, eating their scraps. But there came a point in time that "he came to himself" (Luke 15:17) The people you want to reach need to have that "come to Jesus" moment where they recognize that God provides a better way. A way that not only will set them free of their present circumstances but will run to them to restore the things lost. "...It was right that we should make merry and be glad, for your brother was dead and is alive again, and was lost and is found." (Luke 15:31)

So what does that mean in the practical? It means to speak life over them. Do not constantly bring up where they were or what they did, but instead, speak to who they are to become and who they are in Christ. Recognize, but for the precious blood of Jesus, you would be lost and trapped yourself. Do not try to figure out how God will do it; just trust that IT IS DONE! Remember to not keep rehashing the past, but to encourage them in the future that God has for them. Give them a soft place to fall and turn their lives around. Amen!

In Conclusion

(A Word from the Author)

Hello friends!

First, I just wanted to say how very grateful I am that you took the time to read this book. I set my faith with you that you will see mountains moved and your people restored. As a token of my appreciation, I want to give you a free downloadable of the "Prayer and Confession to rescue the lost, stalked, and prodigals." That way you can put it on your mirrors, refrigerators, or in your Bibles.

Lastly, if you have enjoyed this book and found it useful, would you take a moment and give my book a review to help spread this message of hope to others who need to know that God has made a way for them. Simply click the QR Code below and it will take you to my book link on Amazon where you can leave your review or go to Amazon and search Kerry E. Garner Books and you can find my book and leave a review there.

Please know that my heart is to help you, the way God helped me.

Many blessings,

Kerry E. Garner

Leave a Book Review: **Free Downloadable:**

References

[1]*New King James Version.* Copyright ©1982 by Thomas Nelson, Inc. Strong, J. (2010).

[2]Dutch Sheets. 2021, July 20. How to Pray for the Lost | Give Him 15: Daily Prayer with Dutch. https://www.youtube.com/watch?v=aeReH132QOE&t=149s

[3]*Strong, J. (2010) The New Strong's Expanded Exhaustive Concordance of the Bible* (Red-letter ed.). Thomas Nelson. Edition #1. Used by permission. All rights reserved.

[4]A Sermon (No. 2246) Intended for Reading on Lord's-Day, March 6th, 1892, Delivered by C. H. SPURGEON, At the Metropolitan Tabernacle, Newington On Thursday Evening, May 15th, 1890.

[5]*Amplified® Bible Classic Edition.* Copyright © 1954, 1958, 1962, 1964, 1965, 1987 by The Lockman Foundation. Used by permission.

About the Author:
Kerry E. Garner

Kerry E. Garner is an author dedicated to her faith, family, community, and country. Growing up in the beautiful South Arkansas town of Hamburg, Kerry was provided a fertile ground that enriched and nurtured her love of God. She graduated from Oral Roberts University with a degree in English Literature. She married the love of her life, Frank Garner, in 1990, and they raised two incredible sons. Kerry founded a faith-based women's Bible study in 2000, a steadfast endeavor through which she continues to impart the teachings of God to this day. Over the course of two decades, Kerry served her church, offering comfort, encouragement, and a prayer of faith for those in the hospital and those needing altar ministry, where she also served as team lead. Today, she dedicates herself to her family, ladies' ministry, the healing ministry and prayer with Loudmouth Prayer, attends daily morning prayer, and is an active member of Victory Church serving on the dream team as an altar counselor. She continues to study God's word and looks forward to writing more books. Kerry is available for women's ministry speaking engagements and can be contacted at kerryegarner@gmail.com.

Testimonials of breakthrough can be sent to the same email address or sent on messenger to @kerryelisabethgarner on Instagram.

Additional books by this author can be found on Amazon.com under Kerry E. Garner Books: Children's Book:

The Adventure Series:

Brandon and Brad's Backyard Adventure

Brandon and Brad's Water Park Adventure

Brandon and Brad's Pirate Ship Adventure

Brandon and Brad's Grandparent Adventure

Brandon and Brad's Italian Family's Adventure in Buffalo, NY

With the Animals and Me Series:

Come ABC with the Animals and Me

Come 123 with the Animals and Me

Princess Fluffy Toes Loves to Dance

When Jenny Met Jesus: A Prayer of Salvation for Children

Psalms 23 for Children: Empowered to face Fears, Bullies and Life in the Real World

www.ingramcontent.com/pod-product-compliance
Lightning Source LLC
Chambersburg PA
CBHW062018040426
42447CB00010B/2043